1 MONTH OF
FREE
READING

at

www.ForgottenBooks.com

By purchasing this book you are eligible for one month membership to ForgottenBooks.com, giving you unlimited access to our entire collection of over 1,000,000 titles via our web site and mobile apps.

To claim your free month visit:

www.forgottenbooks.com/free1303015

ISBN 978-0-428-67924-8
PIBN 11303015

Historic, Archive Document

Do not assume content reflects current
scientific knowledge, policies, or practices.

Management
Methods
Application
Group
Fort Collins,
Colorado 80524

POPULATIONS FOLLOWING THE 1979

CASCADE, IDAHO CONTROL PROJECT

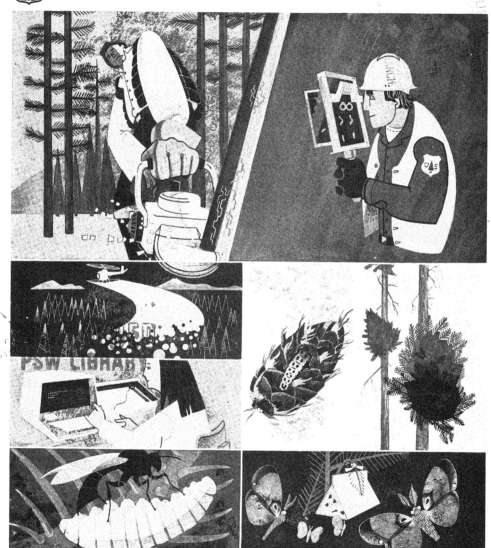

Report No. 85-3

3400
April 1985

STATUS OF WESTERN SPRUCE BUDWORM POPULATIONS FOLLOWING THE
1979 CASCADE, IDAHO CONTROL PROJECT

by

M.A. Marsden[1]/, D.B. Cahill[2]/, and R.L. Livingston[3]/

ABSTRACT

Western spruce budworm population monitoring was conducted as a follow-up to a 1979 central Idaho suppression project. The treatments were acephate, carbaryl and untreated checks. Information collected over the four year period, 1979-1982, included tree tip growth, larvae per one hundred buds, egg masses per meter square, and male moths captured by pheromone trapping. Tree tip growth was not found to be greatly influenced by budworm defoliation. Budworm populations, as measured by larvae and egg mass densities, were significantly reduced following the spray treatments, but returned to pretreatment densities within the monitoring period.

INTRODUCTION

The western spruce budworm, Choristoneura occidentalis Freeman, is a native insect which has been reported as a pest in North America since the late 1800's (Knopf, et al. 1978). In the Intermountain Region the first epidemic was recorded in southern Idaho in 1922. Since that time, budworm populations have built up to epidemic proportions, and subsided on a somewhat periodic basis (Johnson and Denton 1975). In recent years, epidemics were noted in the 1950's, the early 1960's, and again in the 1970's. Historical records in the Intermountain Region, which encompasses the Boise and Payette National Forests, show infestations of about nine years duration with an upper limit to about 15 years.

The first large scale aerial budworm spray program in the west took place from 1955 to 1957 and included the Boise and Payette National Forests (Johnson et al. 1975). In 1954, when aerial detection programs were begun in the

[1]/Biometrician, USDA Forest Service, Forest Pest Management, Methods Application Group, Fort Collins, CO 80526.
[2]/Entomologist (CANUSA), FPM, Boise Field Office, Region 4, Boise, ID 83702.
[3]/Supervisor, Insect and Disease Section, State of Idaho Department of Lands Coeur d'Alene, ID 83814.

rmountain Region; western spruce budworm defoliation was reported o
ral forests. Activity since that time has been observed on an annua
s with infestations ranging from localized areas to an excess of 2,000,00
s in 1964.

uring 1979, 447,000 acres of southwestern Idaho were defoliated by wester
ce budworm (USDA 1979). Most of this defoliation occurred on land
osed predominantly of high value grand fir habitat types. After a fe
s of heavy defoliation, damage associated with this insect included radia
height growth loss, top kill, tree mortality. Top kill often results i
introduction of decay into dead tops, and loss of cones or cone producin
of trees. This can reduce future Douglas-fir and true fir regeneration.

ne Boise and Payette National Forests decided to accelerate the harves
ram on lands containing high rate of return in grand fir in order t
nize budworm caused losses (Hamre 1979).

ne Idaho Department of Lands and Boise Cascade Corporation determined tha
r timber lands needed immediate protection (Livingston et al. 1982).
sion was made in 1979 to conduct the Idaho Cooperative Spruce Budwor
ect on 139,530 acres in Valley and Boise Counties, near the community o
ade (Figure 1). There would be no spraying of National Forest land
ot for minimum buffer strips to assure coverage of adjacent state an
ate lands.

ne treatment area was divided into northern and southern units. A
eated check area was designated for each of these units for compariso
ses. The northern unit was divided into the Gold Fork, Patty Flat an
Creek subunits; the south unit into the Packer John, West Mountain an
1's Ferry subunits. Each subunit was further divided into spray block
aging 3,000 acres. Each spray block was uniquely numbered to facilitat
ing track of sample data and scheduling of spray operations.

vo insecticides were used in the project, carbaryl (Sevin-4-oil®),
imate compound; and acephate (Orthene Forest Spray®)[4/], a
lophosphate compound. The carbaryl was used in the southern unit and i
spray blocks of the northern unit. Acephate was used in the northern uni
to treat a protective buffer around designated streams, ponds, an
.tive areas in the southern area. Non-spray buffer zones were also lef
ortions of seven streams in the northern unit and on portions of nin
ams in the southern unit. The non-spray buffer zone consisted of a 200
no-treatment zone on each side of the specified streams in the norther
and a 400 foot no-treatment zone on each side of the designate

---

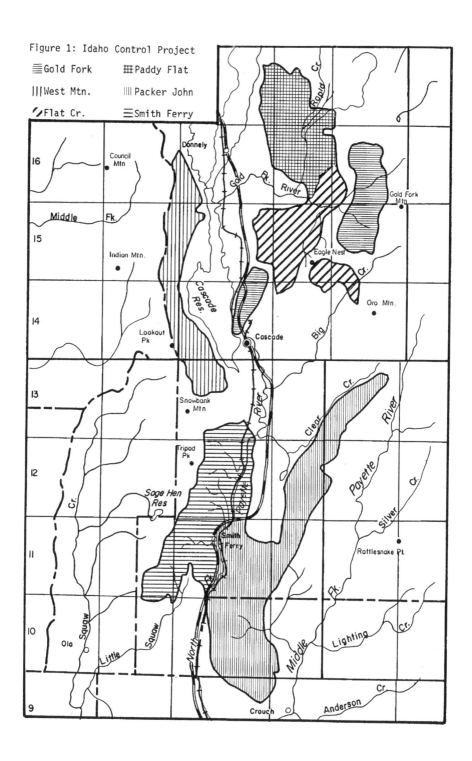

Figure 1: Idaho Control Project

≣ Gold Fork   ▦ Paddy Flat

||| West Mtn.   ⫴ Packer John

⟋ Flat Cr.   ≡ Smith Ferry

streams in the southern unit except for the North Fork of the Payette River which had a 200 foot no-spray area within the designated zone.

METHODS

The population monitoring project was conducted to determine the duration of treatment effects, i.e., how long might it take for the western spruce budworm population to once again build up to epidemic levels in the treated area. It was also hoped that we could determine if a buildup was due to resurgence from individuals that survived the treatment or to reinvasion from surrounding untreated areas.

One-hundred and fifty 3-tree sampling clusters were established at random throughout the area, 25 in each subunit. The clusters were located at least 100 yards inside the spray boundary and 100 feet from roads. The sample trees were Douglas-fir or true firs, 35-50 feet tall, with previous defoliation not exceeding 25 percent. The clusters were numbered individually and used for all sampling in each of the four years (1979-1982).

Four measurements were taken on each plot relating to the western spruce budworm: larval density (larvae/100 buds); egg mass density (eggs/square meter of foliage); pheromone sticky trap catches of male moths; and tip-growth data. Measurements taken in 1979 included data for both pre- and post-spray populations and tree growth. The basic effect of the treatment was measured by the change in larval density following treatment. Annual measurements of larval and egg mass densities demonstrate population recovery through time when measured once each year. Moth trap density measures another aspect of the budworm population recovery through time. The tip growth data is a measure of budworm impact.

Analyses of variance and paired comparisons of means were made for each measurement for each year. Differences by year and through time were noted. Statistical tests for relationships among measurements and through time were conducted.

RESULTS

LARVAL DENSITY - The effect of the treatments was measured by larval density before and after application. The units did not differ significantly, alpha = 0.05, in larval density before treatment but did differ following treatment (Tables 1 and 2). Each of the spray treatments did, in fact, reduce the population levels of western spruce budworm.

An overview of the larval density by area (subunit) through time is seen in Figure 2. A separate analysis of variance for each time period presented in Figure 2 is found in Table 3. It is not sufficient to know that some areas have a statistically different larval density than the others. Estimates of the density by area and tests of significance between particular areas are needed to evaluate the project.

Table 1: Larvae Density (larvae/100 buds) in 1979 Pre-Treatment by
          Treatment Areas

Analysis of Variance Table

Source	Degrees of Freedom	Sum of Squares	Mean Squares	F (P)[1]
Treatment	2	322.32	161.16	0.55 (>.250)
Areas/T	3	874.71	291.57	
Samples/A/T	136	12,104.19	89.00	
Total	141	13,301.22		

Treatment	Average Larvae Density
	[2]
Carbaryl	14.83
Acephate	16.42
Check	13.11

[1]/P is the probability of an F value this large or larger when treatments
are not different.

[2]/Treatment means connected by the same line are not significantly
different at the Alpha = 0.05 levels using "t" test with separate variances.

Table 2: Larvae Density (Larvae/100 Buds) in 1979 Post-Treatment by
          Treatment Areas

Analysis of Variance Table

Source	Degrees of Freedom	Sum of Squares	Mean Squares	F (P)[1]
Treatment	2	801.56	400.79	9.31 (<.050)
Areas/T	3	129.9	43.03	
Samples/A/T	136	997.42		
Total	141	1,928.07		

Treatment	Average Larvae Density
	[2]
Carbaryl	0.43
Acephate	1.73
Check	6.44

[1]/P is the probability of an F value this large or larger when treatments
are not different.

[2]/Treatment means connected by the same line are not significantly
different at the Alpha = 0.05 levels using "t" test with separate variances.

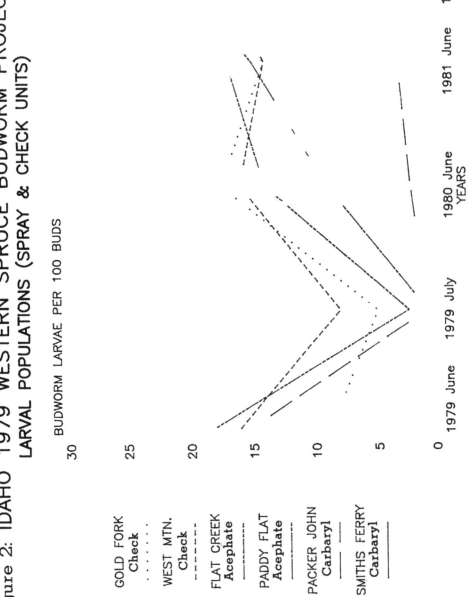

Figure 2: IDAHO 1979 WESTERN SPRUCE BUDWORM PROJECT LARVAL POPULATIONS (SPRAY & CHECK UNITS)

In addition to our need for more detailed information than that given in Table 3, is the question of homogeneous variance within areas. This assumption is necessary for testing in the analysis of variance. It has been found by others (Walton and DeMars 1973) and was observed here, that homogeneity is not found when the larval density varies greatly among units, as it does in the 1980 data set. To account for these problems, individual pairs of density measurements were tested for areas within each time period. Between every pair of means a "t" test, using separate variance (Welch) tests was computed (Brown and Forsythe 1974). To adjust for the large number of comparisons the Bonferroni probabilities were used, giving a simultaneous significant level, alpha = 0.05 (Bohrer and others 1981). In Table 4, the density by areas and time periods are presented with the significant difference between pairs indicated.

Flat Creek had a significantly higher population density (larvae) than Gold Fork prior to treatment. No other pair-wise differences were detected prior to treatment (Table 4).

Following treatment the larval population in Packer John and Smith Ferry decreased greatly to fewer than one larva per 100 buds (Table 4). Each area was significantly less than the density in either check area, West Mountain or Gold Fork. The Paddy Flat area with a larval density of 1.12 larvae per 100 buds was also significantly less than the check areas. Flat Creek, with a larval density of 2.33/100 buds, was significantly less in density to only the West Mountain check area. Flat Creek and Gold Fork were not significantly different. It should be remembered here that in the pretreatment sampling Flat Creek had the highest, and Gold Fork the lowest, population densities. Post treatment Flat Creek density was less than half that of Gold Fork.

During 1980, 1981, and 1982 samples were taken to coincide with the pretreatment samples in 1979, on each of the six areas. In the 1980 sampling Packer John and Smith Ferry were significantly lower in density than any of the other four areas (Figure 2, Table 4). Their densities of 1.33 and 1.11 per 100 buds, were significantly different from the untreated checks, Gold Fork and West Mountain (17.39 and 15.55 larvae per 100 buds respectively). The Paddy Flat area with a larval density of 8.60/100 buds, also was significantly lower in density than either check area. Flat Creek, however, with a density of 12.25 larvae per 100 buds, was not significantly different from either the West Mountain or Gold Fork check areas.

In the 1981 sampling, population reduction due to the acephate treatment were no longer apparent (Figure 2, Table 4). The two areas treated with carbaryl had also begun to show population increases. Packer John had a density of 3.42 larvae/100 buds and Smith Ferry a density of 3.16. These were still significantly lower than any of the other four areas; however, those other areas ranged from 12.10 to 17.14 larvae per 100 buds. No significant differences were found among these four areas.

By 1982 population densities in all areas except Packer John had risen to or beyond the pretreatment levels of 1979. The density of 10.98 for Packer John was still significantly lower than the other areas except Smith Ferry (Table 4).

Table 3: Analysis of Variance Tables for WSBW Larval Density for
Each of Five Time Periods by Treatment Areas

	Source	Degrees of Freedom	Sum of Squares	Mean Squares	F (P) [1]
Pre-	Areas	5	1,197.03	239.41	2.69 (<.050)
Treatment	Within/A	136	12,104.19	89.00	
1979	Total	141	13,301.22		
Post-	Areas	5	930.65	186.13	25.01 (<.005)
Treatment	Within/A	134	997.42	7.44	
1979	Total	139	1,928.07		
1980	Areas	5	5,416.51	1,083.30	21.93 (<.005)
	Within/A	131	6,470.31	49.39	
	Total	136	11,886.82		
1981	Areas	5	4,358.62	871.72	24.63 (<.005)
	Within/A	137	4,849.13	35.40	
	Total	142	9,207.75		
1982	Areas	5	3,396.07	679.21	7.55 (<.005)
	Within/A	137	12,321.05	89.93	
	Total	142	15,717.12		

[1]/P is the probability of an F value this large or larger when Areas are not
different.

Table 4: Pairwise comparisons of Larvae Density/100 Buds for Each
Time Period by Treatment Areas

Pre-Treatment 1979 [1] [2]		Post-Treatment 1979		1980	
A Flat C.	18.86	N West M.	7.28	N Gold F.	17.39
N West M.	16.43	N Gold F.	5.24	N West M.	15.55
C Packer J.	15.82	A Flat C.	2.33	A Flat C.	12.25
A Paddy F.	13.97	A Paddy F.	1.12	A Paddy F.	8.60
C Smith F.	13.88	C Packer J.	0.44	C Packer J.	1.33
N Gold F.	8.92	C Smith F.	0.43	C Smith F.	1.11

1981		1982	
A Flat C.	17.14	A Flat C.	25.39
A Paddy F.	15.34	A Paddy F.	24.20
N Gold F.	12.22	N Gold F.	22.34
N West M.	12.10	N West M.	19.18
C Packer J.	3.42	C Smith F.	17.57
C Smith F.	3.16	C Packer J.	10.98

[1]/C = Carbaryl; A = Acephate; N = Non-treatment check
[2]/Areas connected by the same line are not significantly different at the
Alpha = .05 level, using "t" tests with separate variances.

EGG MASSES — Egg mass data collected in the fall of 1979, 1980, 1981, and 1982 was subjected to analysis of variance and pair-wise comparison of means similar to the analysis of the larval density data (Figure 3, Table 6).

An examination of the analyses of variance Table 5 and pair-wise comparisons, Table 6, reveals significant difference in areas that could be interpreted as treatment effect in 1979 but disappear by 1982. The primary effect found was a low egg mass density in the areas treated with carbaryl for three years following treatment.

In 1979 the areas of greatest egg mass density were Gold Fork (4.178 e.m./m^2) and West Mountain (3.624 e.m./m^2). These values were significantly greater than the densities at Packer John (1.021 e.m./m^2) or Smith Ferry (1.088 e.m./m^2). The areas Flat Creek (2.840 e.m./m^2) and Paddy Flat (2.489 e.m./m^2) were intermediate in egg mass density and not significantly different from any of the other areas.

In 1980, again a high, low, and intermediate grouping of the areas by egg mass density occured. Flat Creek joined West Mountain and Gold Fork to form the high density group. Packer John and Smith Ferry remained as the low density group and the lone intermediate value was Paddy Flat. The low density areas were significantly different from the high density areas. Due to unequal sampling density the intermediate area, Paddy Flat, was significantly different from only one high density area, Gold Fork.

In 1981 conditions were very similar to 1980. Flat Creek, Gold Fork and West Mountain form a high density group (9.633–16.828 e.m./m^2). Smith Ferry and Packer John were the low density group. Paddy Flat was again intermediate. Areas in the low density group were significantly different from the areas in the high density group and Paddy Flat. Paddy Flat also was significantly different from Flat Creek in the high density group.

By 1982 there was no low density group. All egg mass densities were greater than the largest densities found in 1979 or 1980. Flat Creek, with a density of 16.180 e.m./m^2 was significantly greater than Paddy Flat, Smith Ferry, Packer John, or West Mountain. Gold Fork, the next greatest density was significantly greater than Smith Ferry, Packer John, and West Mountain. The rise in egg mass density in the two carbaryl treated areas and the decline in density in the check area, West Mountain, resulted in an end to any detectable treatment effects.

ADULT TRAP DATA — Traps to catch male moths were deployed in 1980, 1981, and 1982. The sampling was not as uniform as for the larvae and egg masses. For example, no trapping was done in West Mountain in 1980, and only two traps were used in Packer John in each year. In general, the other areas had 20–25 traps per area each year. Differences were found among areas but they did not fit the pattern expected due to treatments (Tables 7 and 8). In 1980 only by pooling the variances could one significant difference be found using pair-wise comparisons of the area means. Flat Creek had significantly greater male moth catch than Smith Ferry. Due to smaller sample sizes in the other areas, significant differences could not be found.

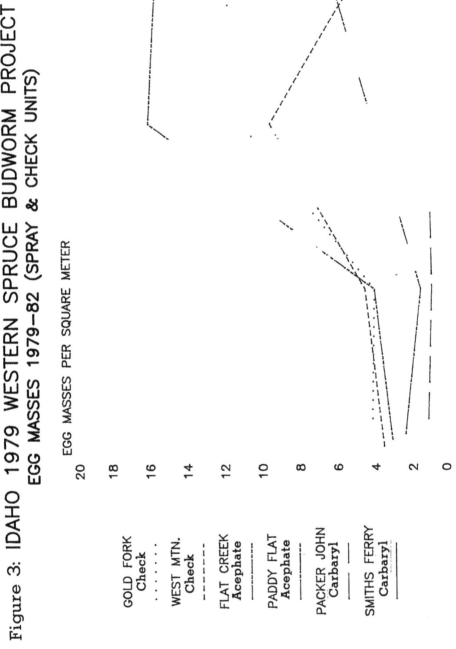

Figure 3: IDAHO 1979 WESTERN SPRUCE BUDWORM PROJECT
EGG MASSES 1979–82 (SPRAY & CHECK UNITS)

EGG MASSES PER SQUARE METER

GOLD FORK
Check

WEST MTN.
Check

FLAT CREEK
Acephate

PADDY FLAT
Acephate

PACKER JOHN
Carbaryl

SMITHS FERRY
Carbaryl

Table 5: Analysis of Variance Tables for Egg Mass Densities
for 1979 to 1982 by Treatment Areas

Year	Source	Degrees of Freedom	Sum of Squares	Mean Squares	F (P)[1]
1979	Areas	5	181.87	36.37	6.20 (<.005)
	Within A	131	768.20	5.86	
	Total	136	950.07		
1980	Areas	5	492.55	98.51	8.31 (<.005)
	Within A	119	1,410.40	11.85	
	Total	124	1,902.95		
1981	Areas	5	4,816.14	963.23	14.25 (<.005)
	Within A	138	9,328.52	67.60	
	Total	143	14,144.66		
1982	Areas	5	2,498.05	499.61	17.41 (<.005)
	Within A	137	3,931.28	28.69	
	Total	142	6,429.32		

[1]/P is the probability of an F value this large or larger when Areas are not
different.

Table 6: Pairwise Comparisons of Egg Mass Density for Each Year
by Treatment Areas

Treatment
Code   1979

[1]/		[2]/
N Gold F.	4.178	
N West M.	3.624	
A Flat C.	2.840	
A Paddy F.	2.487	
C Packer J.	1.021	
C Smith F.	1.088	

1980

N West M.	4.814
A Flat C.	4.654
N Gold F.	4.117
A Paddy F.	1.267
C Packer J.	0.508
C Smith F.	0.168

1981

A Flat C.	16.828
N Cold F.	11.143
N West M.	9.633
A Paddy F.	5.028
C Smith F.	1.060
C Packer J.	0.833

1982

A Flat C.	16.180
N Gold F.	12.500
A Paddy F.	7.920
C Smith F.	5.804
C Packer J.	5.308
N West M.	5.108

[1]/C = Carbaryl; A = Acephate; N = Non-treatment check
[2]/Areas connected with the same line are not significantly different at
Alpha = 0.05 level using "t" tests with separate variances.

Table 7: Analysis of Variance Tables for Moth Trap Data for 1980 to 1982 by Treatment Areas

Year	Source	Degrees of Freedom	Sum of Squares	Mean Squares	F (P)[1]
1980	Areas	4	102,581.79	25,645.44	3.29 (<.025)
	Within A	73	568,652.58	7,789.76	
	Total	77	671,234.37		
1981	Areas	5	145,352.04	29,070.41	5.21 (<.005)
	Within A	112	625,345.35	5,583.44	
	Total	117	770,697.39		
1982	Areas	5	1,166,262.81	233,252.56	15.09 (<.005)
	Within A	110	1,700,732.28	15,461.20	
	Total	115	2,866,995.09		

[1]/P is the probability of an F value this large or larger when Areas are not different.

Table 8: Pairwise Comparisons of Total Moths Caught Per Trap for 1980, 1981, and 1982 by Treatment Areas

1980[1]	[2]/	1981		1982	
A Flat C.	225.71	A Paddy F.	290.73	A Paddy F.	411.82
N Smith F.	149.79	N West M.	278.44	A Flat C.	406.24
C Smith F.	142.44	A Flat C.	267.64	C Smith F.	400.96
A Paddy E.	138.87	C Smith F.	261.04	N Gold F.	270.26
C Packer J.	80.00	N Gold F.	186.68	C Packer J.	179.50
		C Packer J.	180.00	N West M.	163.83

[1]/C = Carbaryl; A = Acephate; N = Non-treatment check
[2]/Areas connected with the same line are not significantly different at Alpha = 0.05 level using "t" tests with separate variances.

The number of male moths trapped in 1981 was much higher than 1980. The high count group consisted of Paddy Flat, West Mountain, Flat Creek and Smith Ferry (Table 8). Gold Fork, with a low trap count of 186.68, was significantly less than any member of the high count group. Packer John had an average catch of 180, but this was from two traps and was not significantly different from the high group or from Gold Fork, due to small sample size.

In 1982 average catch of male moths climbed still higher in Paddy Flat, Flat Creek and Smith Ferry (Table 8), to the 400 range. Counts at Gold Fork, Packer John and West Mountain were lower. Of these, West Mountain was also significantly lower than Gold Fork. It should be noted that Gold Fork and West Mountain are the two check areas.

TIP GROWTH DATA - Tip growth is a host effect measurement rather than a budworm population measurement. It was also highly variable between areas. Part of this variation may have been due to budworm feeding, but there were other environmental factors to be considered such as rainfall, summer temperature, and stand development. In addition, budworm feeding may have had a delayed effect, depending on the temperature and precipitation experienced.

The analysis of variance (Table 9) detected significant differences in tip growth by area in each of the four years. In 1979 much of the tip growth should have occurred before treatment. In this year the only significant difference was between Packer John and Flat Creek (Table 10).

In 1980 a pattern of tip growth by area was detected that related to the treatments imposed. Packer John and Smith Ferry had the greatest tip growth rates. These were the carbaryl treated areas; however, they were not significantly different from West Mountain, a check area, or Flat Creek, an acephate treated area. They were different from Paddy Flat and Gold Fork check tip growth rates.

The 1980 pattern changed in 1981. Packer John again had the greatest tip growth rate. This was true in 1979 before expression of treatments was expected as well as for 1980. In fact, Packer John had the greatest tip growth each year of measurement. In 1981 Packer John was significantly greater than only Paddy Flat. The second best growth rate was observed at West Mountain, a check area.

In 1982 a clear pattern following treatment expectations was found; however, it was not supported by appropriate levels of significance, (Table 10). Packer John had superior tip growth compared to either check area. Smith Ferry had significantly greater tip growth than one check area, West Mountain. The remaining comparisons are not supported by statistical significance.

Further analysis of the tip growth on the Idaho cooperative western spruce budworm data was completed. Selecting only those samples of the original 25 in each area with complete data for larvae and tip growth for 1979, 1980, 1981, and 1982, two additional variables were than calculated: the sum of 1980 and 1981 tip growth; and the sum of 1980, 1981, and 1982 tip growth.

e 9: Analysis of Variance Tables for Tip Growth Data for
      1979 to 1982 by Treatment Areas

urce	Degrees of Freedom	Sum of Squares	Mean Squares	F (]
eas	5	3,792.20	758.44	3.82 (
thin A	111	22,025.53	198.43	
tal	116	25,817.73		
eas	5	6,779.55	1,355.91	4.40 (
thin A	120	36,961.63	308.01	
tal	125	43,741.18		
eas	5	6,641.89	1,328.38	2.51 (
thin A	138	73,058.19	529.41	
tal	143	79,700.08		
eas	5	16,666.63	3,333.32	5.11 (
thin A	137	89,290.16	651.75	
tal	142	105,956.79		

ie probability of an F value this large or larger when Aress are
nt.

---

e 10: Pairwise Comparisons of Tip Growth in cm for 1979 to 198:
       by Treatment Areas

1979		1980		1981	
Units of Measure 2/					
J.	63.05	C Packer J.	69.38	C Packer J.	7]
	55.98	C Smith F.	64.00	N West M.	67
	53.76	N West M.	59.60	A Flat C.	64
.	49.31	A Flat C.	57.99	C Smith F.	62
.	49.28	A Paddy F.	49.52	N Gold F.	56
	45.72	N Gold F.	48.94	A Paddy F.	5]

1982

J.	70.99
'	57.41
	49.62
.	46.53
	43.42
	37.52

baryl; A = Acephate; N = Non-treatment check
onnected with the same line are not significantly different at
0.05 level using "t" tests with separate variances.

The analysis of variance for total tip growth in 1980-81, indicated a significant area effect (Table 11). Total tip growth for 1980-82 also indicated a significant area effect when subject to an analysis of variance. This was not surprising since the individual years of tip growth had shown significant difference in previous analysis using all data available each year.

From the past analysis one would conclude that trees in one area grew differently from those in another, but this difference could not be clearly related to treatment of the area. Thinking that the cumulation of tip growth over time since treatment would show an effect, the new analyses were calculated.

Having again found significant difference in tip growth by area, we examined the means using a series of t-tests to see if a pattern reflecting treatment effects is found. The cumulative growth in areas treated with carbaryl was different from the check areas (alpha = 0.10) and nearly so at the alpha = 0.05 level (Table 12). The negative inference was that the areas treated with acephate, not only do not show growth superiority to the checks, but one area, Paddy Flat, had the lowest growth rate of all areas.

The analysis of covariance was used to examine the individual year's tip growth using tip growth in previous years and larval density as covariates. No consistent patterns were detected. The relationship between the covariates and current year's tip growth varies from area to area and from year to year. These analyses are not included in this report.

EFFECT OF RESURGENCE AND REINVASION - Analysis of larval and egg mass densities has shown that both carbaryl and acephate are effective in reducing western spruce budworm population densities. Carbaryl's effect was greater and lasted longer than that of acephate. However, by 1982 all treated areas had larval density at pretreatment densities or higher.

The spruce budworm populations in the treated areas could have built up from survivors within the area (resurgence), or from immigration of budworm from outside the treated area (reinvasion).

The resurgence vs reinvasion question is not a clear issue. Resurgence is possible as there were at least eight miles of untreated, 200-400 foot, buffer zones left on both sides of designated streams.

It should also be noted when examining the question of resurgence and reinvasion that the actual population density is not the point of interest. The question is only, did the increase through time come from within the area or outside the treated area?

In an attempt to test for the presence of reinvasion, the sample clusters within each treated area were post stratified into an "Interior" group or a

11: Analysis of Variance Cumulated Tip Growth by
Treatment Areas

rce	Degrees of Freedom	Sum of Squares	Mean Squares	F (P)[1]
as	5	20,436.02	4,087.20	3.36 (<.0078)
hin/A	92	111,812.68	1,215.35	
al	97	132,248.70		
as	5	57,056.50	11,411.30	5.26 (<.0003)
hin/A	92	199,489.58	2,168.36	
al	97	256,546.08		

bability of an F value this large or larger when Areas are not

---

12: Pairwise Comparison for Cumulative Tip Growth
in cm by Treatment Areas

1980-81 means	1980-82 means
141.59	214.89
133.91	191.98
124.29	166.44
124.27	159.37
109.56	154.57
100.65	149.92

; A = Acephate; N = Non-treatment check

cted with the same line are not significantly different at
5 level using "t" tests with separate variances.

"Border" group. This gave 12, or often fewer, observations in a group. A non-parametic test using "Rank Sums" was computed to test for population differences between the two groups.

The Smith Ferry area was treated with carbaryl. There were 13 sample clusters identified as "Interior" clusters and 12 identified as "Border" clusters. Using the "Rank Sum" as a statistic the larval density of these groups was not different, therefore, reinvasion does not appear to be a logical explanation of the population increase observed from 1979 to 1982 (Table 13).

The Packer John area was also treated with carbaryl. There were 11 sample clusters identified as "Interior" clusters and 11 identified as "Border" clusters. Three clusters were not used in the nonparametric test due to some missing values. Using the "Rank Sum" as a statistic these groups were found to be different in 1981 Larvae density.

The difference in ranks in 1981 was significant, alpha = 0.0040. Since the "Border" was greater than the "Interior", reinvasion is a possible explanation.

The Paddy Flat area was treated with acephate. There were 13 sample clusters identified as "Interior" clusters and 10 identified as "Border" clusters. Two clusters were deleted from the non-parametric analysis due to missing values. Using the "Rank Sum" as a statistic these groups were found to be different in 1980 Larvae density.

The difference in ranks in 1980 was significant, alpha = .0010. Since the "Border" was greater than the "Interior", reinvasion is a possible explanation. This difference occurred when the budworm population within the area should have been reduced from the acephate treatment.

The Flat Creek area was treated with acephate. There were 13 sample clusters identified as "Interior" clusters and 12 identified as "Border" clusters. Using the "Rank Sum" as a statistic these groups were found to be different in 1982 larvae density.

The difference in ranks in 1982 was significant, alpha = 0.0442. Since the "Interior" was greater than the "Border", reinvasion is not a reasonable explanation. Also, the average density for the area had already reattained it's pretreatment population level, the year before this difference occurred.

It appears that either resurgence or resurgence and reinvasion were operating in the treated area. In either case, budworm populations returned to their pretreatment levels in three years.

Table 13: Tests for Reinvasion of Treated Area
Rank Sum Statistic

		Larval Density	Rank Sums Interior	Border
Smith Ferry				
Pre-treatment	1979	13.884	196.5	128.5
Post-treatment	1979	0.432	183.5	141.5
	1980	1.108	194.5	130.5
	1981	3.160	175.5	149.5
	1982	17.568	158.0	167.0
Packer John				
Pre-treatment	1979	16.100	115.5	137.5
Post-treatment	1979	0.477	126.0	127.0
	1980	1.332	129.5	123.5
	1981	3.404	83.0	170.0
	1982	11.364	108.0	145.0
Paddy Flat				
Pre-treatment	1979	12.935	183.0	93.0
Post-treatment	1979	1.052	134.5	141.5
	1980	8.604	103.0	173.0
	1981	15.656	138.0	138.0
	1982	24.765	163.0	113.0
Flat Creek				
Pre-treatment	1979	18.864	191.0	134.0
Post-treatment	1979	2.528	142.0	183.0
	1980	12.252	152.0	173.0
	1981	17.140	171.0	154.0
	1982	25.392	206.0	119.0

[1]/P equals the probability of this difference in ranks or difference when the two areas are equal.

DISCUSSION

Reduced tip growth of branches is not totally an effect of spruce budworm defoliation. Some areas have apparently different growth rates due to factors other than the budworm.

The analysis of larval and egg mass densities for the 1979 pre- and post-spray population measurements confirm the observations of Livingston et al (1982), that both carbaryl and acephate, used operationally, are effective in reducing western spruce budworm populations to levels that have been judged acceptable. For both pesticides, the post-spray larval population was below the 2.1-3.0 larvae/100 buds used as a standard for measuring effectiveness of control by the USDA Forest Service, Region 6 (USDA-FS 1976) and well below the population level of 5 larvae or less/100 buds used in a 1977 pilot project for acephate (Stipe et al. 1977). The fact that the larval population increased to match or exceed pre-spray populations within three years after the spray is very significant. While analysis of the data does not provide a definitive answer as to the source of the population buildup, it does suggest that both resurgence and reinvasion have contributed. This is especially the case in the area treated with acephate where the population recovered to pre-spray levels one year after treatment in the Flat Creek subunit and after two years in the Paddy Flat subunit. This may be due to the acephate area having the highest post spray population, thus allowing for resurgence, and it was the least like a complete entomological unit which could allow for reinvasion.

Irregardless of the reason, under the conditions encountered in the 1979 Idaho spray project, the duration of effectiveness was three years at best, and less than that for portions of the project area.

In each decision to conduct an operational spray project the question of duration of treatment effect is asked. In Washington and Oregon no surviving larval population of less than 7.5 larvae/100 buds has ever been reported to resurge to epidemic proportions (USDA-FS, 1976). In a New Mexico project carbaryl was aerially applied to a building western spruce budworm population in an isolated mountain range. After three years the population, while increasing slightly, remained at low levels. Resurgence was first observed in the fourth year and continued to increase exceeding pretreatment levels in the sixth year (USDA 1977; Telfer 1984). In these situations treatment of entire entomological units or isolated stands apparently enhanced the treatment effectiveness.   In the Idaho project, treatments were neither of isolated areas nor of complete entomological units.

To better detect the presence of reinvasion would require more intensive sampling and a revised sampling design. Ten or more sample clusters at each of five specified distances from the border, and no untreated zones within the areas, would allow for a more critical assessment. This would also double the sampling effort.

REFERENCES

Bohrer, R., C. Winston, R. Faith, V.M. Joshi and C.-F. Wu. 1981. Multiple three-decision rules for factorial simple effects: Bonferroni wins again! J. American Stat. Assoc., March 1981, Vol. 76, No. 373, p. 119-124.

Brown, M.B. and A.B. Forsythe. 1974. The small sample behavior of some statistics which test the equality of several means. Technometrics, Vol. 16, No. 1. Feb. 1974, p.129-132.

Hamre, Vern. 1979. Record of Decision. Western spruce budworm amended final environmental statement Boise and Payette NF, state and private cooperation. Intermountain Region, USDA Forest Service, 1 pp.

Johnson, P.C. and R.E. Denton. 1975. Outbreaks of the western spruce budworm in the American northern Rocky Mountain area from 1922 through 1971. USDA Forest Service Gen. Tech. Rpt. INT-20, 145 pp.

Knopf, J.E., A. Valcarce and R. Beveridge. 1978. Biological evaluation, western spruce budworm, Payette and Boise National Forests, 1977. Forest Service FI&PM, Boise, ID. Rpt. 78-1, 8 pp.

Knopf, J.A.E., R.L. Beveridge and A. Valcarce. 1979. Biological evaluation, western spruce budworm, Boise and Payette National Forests, 1978. Feb. 1979. R-4, 79-2, 8 pp.

Livingston, R.L., J.W. Schwandt, J. Preston, W. Ciesla, B. Davidek, D. Beckman, L. Spickelmire, and R. Johnson. 1982. 1979 Western spruce budworm control project, Cascade, Idaho. Idaho Dept. of Lands Rpt. No. 82-4, 64 pp.

Ollieu, M.M., R.L. Livingston and W.E. Bousfield. 1976. Western spruce budworm impact evaluation, Payette and Boise National Forests and Idaho Department of Lands. USDA Forest Service, Insect and Disease Control, Boise, ID. Rpt. R-4, 77-3, 9 pp.

Ragenovich, I.R. and D.L. Parker. 1981. Western spruce budworm suppression and evalkuation project using carbaryl, 1980. Progress Report No. 4. USDA Forest Service, State and Private Forestry, Southwestern Region. R-3, 81-9, 43 pp.

Stipe, L.E., J.A.E. Knopf, R.L. Livingston, R.W. Young, and G.P. Markin. 1977. A cooperative pilot project with Orthene for control of the western spruce budworm, Choristoneura occidentalis Freeman (Lepidoptera: Torticidae). McCall, Idaho. Forest Service, USDA; State of Idaho:Boise Cascade Corp. 34 pp.

Telfer, William G. 1984. Western spruce budworm suppression and evaluation project using carbaryl, 1977. Progress Rpt. No. 7. USDA Forest Service, State and Private Forestry, Southwestern Region. R-3, 11 pp.

USDA. 1977. Final environmental statement for western spruce budworm suppression and evaluation, Santa Fe National Forest. USDA-FS-R3-FIDM FES ADM 77-03, 132 pp.

USDA. 1978. Western spruce budworm final environmental statement, Boise and Payette National Forests, state and private cooperation. March 1978. Intermountain Region, USDA Forest Service. 148 pp.

USDA. 1979. Western spruce budworm amended final environmental statement Boise and Payette National Forests, state and private cooperation. April 1979. Intermountain Region, USDA Forest Service, 90 pp.

Walton, G.S. and C.J. DeMers. 1973. Empirical methods in the evaluation of estimators, a case study based on insect density and survival data. USDA Forest Service Res. Paper NE-272, 1973. Northeastern Forest Experiment Station, Upper Darby, PA, 15 pp.

USDA-FS, Anon. 1976. Department of Agriculture, Forest Service USDA Environmental Statement, Cooperative western spruce budworm pest management plan. April 1976. USDA, Forest Service. Pacific Northwest Region, 126 pp.